The **28 Day**
TAME YOUR
TEMPER
Parenting
CHALLENGE

The 28 Day

TAME YOUR TEMPER

Parenting CHALLENGE

ISBN: 978-0-9875433-0-1

TABLE OF CONTENTS

INTRODUCTION
HOW TO USE THE 28 DAY
TAME YOUR TEMPER CHALLENGE

I'm the author of *The Happy Mum Handbook* and a life coach specialising in educating clients on how to end stress, depression and anxiety. I teach parents how to understand the thinking that lies behind some of the intense emotions we can experience as parents, and how to change our perspective of the challenging situations that seem to cause them.

We are often told as mums and dads that in order to avoid getting angry or stressed, we should 'walk away when angry' or 'take time out'. But we've heard all this before. I mean, it is valid advice but sometimes it's not enough to stop those emotional outbursts that most often end in guilt and self-criticism.

What I teach instead is some real tools for identifying the specific thoughts that lie behind your stress, and how to change your mindset so you don't get consumed by your emotions and your reactions to life's ups and downs.

Those who are familiar with my work know that I never advocate myself as being a perfect mother with a perfect mindset who never gets stressed by motherhood. Aside of the results I get and the experience I have working with clients suffering with stress, depression and anxiety; what makes me worthy of teaching this information is that I have to apply these very methods to myself everyday!

1

The 28 Day **TAME YOUR TEMPER** CHALLENGE

Many of you even know the story from *The Happy Mum Handbook* where I got so angry one day that I slammed a knife down on the kitchen bench so hard that it bounced off and almost hit my then two-year-old in the head. Not one of my proudest moments, but one of the most influential moments that completely changed the course of my life and led me to being able to teach you how to stop your anger.

The 28 Day Tame Your Temper Challenge was a concept born from my own desire to be a parent who tames her temper and stops the habit of yelling when things don't go my way.

While everyone is different, the idea behind this challenge is that it takes 21 days to break a habit, with a further 7 days to reinforce the new one.

This challenge is about taking 28 days to LEARN how to break the habit of being a parent who tends to yell, shout, or scream the house down.

I highlight the word LEARN because I don't want you to think that you have failed if you don't tame your temper for the entire 28 days.

It's important to remember that we are breaking a habit (to yell and get angry) and learning a new one (to be a calmer parent). Often, when learning a new skill, we do it wrong or make mistakes. This IS moving towards the goal.

How do we know what to do until we have experienced what NOT to do?

So during this challenge, please be gentle on yourself and recognise that change comes with continual repetition, practice and awareness of what you are doing. This is how you learnt to walk, talk, use a spoon, run, jump and even think the way that you presently do.

You will learn to tame your temper using the exact same process – repetition, practice and awareness of what you are doing.

HOW IT WORKS:

Use this book as a daily instruction manual. You'll read new information each day. This should only take about 5-10 minutes, depending on how fast you read. You'll receive the information you need to begin making changes to the way you handle each day's challenges.

This makes it very easy to incorporate new learning into your day. Time is never about time, it's about priorities. Are you going to make it a priority to keep learning how to tame your temper?

This book is providing you with the tools to change. All you need to do is make it a priority to read the material and apply the information.

THE RULES:

You must create, write and sign a written commitment to yourself about your intentions for the 28-day challenge (e.g. "I commit to actively practising the skill of remaining calm, regardless of what challenges I encounter, and promise to learn from any slip-ups I have.").

- Make your agreement something you are likely to commit to for the 28 days.

3

- Place this agreement somewhere around the house for you to see often.

- Let others know about your commitment. Ask them to help you keep to this commitment by letting you know when you are starting to 'lose the plot'.

If/when you drop the ball you must look at what happened and what you were thinking at the time. Learn from what happened and then write your insights into your daily journal.

a) Knowing you have to write about it gives you accountability and makes you less likely to lose it.

b) Writing about it helps you to learn from the minor detour so you can establish a different way to behave next time.

Recognise your wins. Keep a journal of all the wins that you have as you recognise them. While it's important to learn from our mistakes, it is equally important to recognise your wins and give yourself a pat on the back.

WHAT TO DO IF YOU 'DROP THE BALL'?

It is quite common for most of us to go back to old habits and to slip up when trying to change one. This may happen a few times.....or a lot, to begin with. As mentioned, this is not an indication of failure. The important thing to remember is that if you do drop the ball, be sure to learn from it. Look at what was happening for you at the time. Use what you have learnt so far in your daily reading to understand what happened to cause your anger and what you might do differently next time.

MOVE TOWARDS THE GOAL OF TAMING YOUR TEMPER

This challenge has been specifically designed for you to have a progressive, gradient approach to taming your temper.

Rome wasn't built in a day. It took some time to create the thinking that lies behind your angry reactions and it's going to take some time for you to retrain the brain to react differently. However, the good news is that the brain is very clever and can do this rather quickly. It's really quite simple. The more you apply the information you learn, the quicker the brain learns to form the habit of tamingyour temper.

THE FOUR STAGES OF THE TAME YOUR TEMPER CHALLENGE

Each week has been separated into stages of learning and growth, with each week adding onto the previous one. This progressive approach gives you the skills needed to get better and better at taming your temper.

WEEK ONE - Understanding Your Anger

We can't change what we don't acknowledge. We need to become aware of where we are presently before we can begin to change it.

This week is about explaining the real cause of your anger/ frustration and how to recognise the specific thinking that causes your stress. You'll be surprised to learn that it's not your child's behaviour, or any other event.

WEEK TWO – The Shift to Reality

After learning how to recognise the rogue thoughts underlying your stress, this week teaches you how to change this thinking.

You will learn how to accept the reality of the challenging events and shift your perspective of the situation away from stressful thoughts.

WEEK THREE – Let's Get Solution-Focussed

This week, as you may guess, is all about solutions! We so often look for what we aren't getting and how bad things are, but we are not often looking for what to do about these situations.

Week Three is about learning new ways of responding to those little instances that end up sending us over the edge. It's also about seeking out solutions to those bigger behavioural issues that can be quite frustrating.

WEEK FOUR – The Continual Road to Successful Tame Your Temper Parenting

Finally, we get to our last week, where I will introduce you to my 5-step Mind TRACK to Happiness Process that you can apply to ANY situation that causes you stress. It's a great tool, no matter what is happening in your life – regarding parenthood, or any other event.

Finally, I wish you all the best with this challenge. Every one of us has the capacity to change with commitment, practice and application of this information. So it will be up to your persistence as to whether you get the results you are looking for.

The 28 Day **TAME YOUR TEMPER** CHALLENGE

Feel free to email me at info@parentalstress.com.au if you have any questions or would like to comment on how you are going.

Kind Regards,

Jackie Hall
Author of The Happy Mum Handbook
www.parentalstress.com.au

WEEK ONE:
Understanding Your ANGER

DAY 1
WHAT CAUSES ANGER

All stress is a conflict between belief and reality.

The belief is what your opinion, judgement and conversation is about what's happening. Reality is what is actually happening.

When your thinking is not in alignment with what is actually happening, you will likely experience some form of stress.

Often we believe it's events that cause us to feel stressed. "If 'x' wasn't happening, then I wouldn't feel stressed." So we often believe that the answer is to control or manage the situation better.

However, while we will never stop trying to avoid unpleasant situations, the reality is that there are going to be times where they happen anyway, and this was not due to your lack of ability to control a situation. It was due to the reality that life is full of ups and downs, challenges and easy rides, things going to plan and things not going to plan; and parenting is no different.

But if we continue to believe that in order to avoid stress, we need situations to be different (i.e. always go our own way), we will continue to search for a stress-free life that never eventuates.

Let's consider this: If it were the events of life going 'wrong' that caused you to feel stress, then that would mean everyone who experienced that same event, would feel stressed, but we know this isn't entirely true.

Most of us know of a seemingly natural born mum or dad who seems to handle these same events with ease, not really too fazed by the very events that seem to leave you completely flying off the handle.

Similarly, you would know from speaking with other parents that some things happen with their kids that they get really worked up about, but wouldn't really faze you and vice versa.

If different parents are handling challenging situations with their kids with varying levels of stress, or no stress at all, then it can't be the events.

When you think about it, there is another common denominator in your stress other than your children - and that is you!

The ONLY reason why you and other parents are experiencing your stress differently is because each parent perceives these events with a different mindset.

When you change how you think about challenging situations, you will change how you feel about them.

For example:

Parent A may perceive a tantrum from their toddler as learning behaviour. Their child is simply learning how to behave in the world and realising that they can't get what they want.

Parent B may be perceiving how embarrassing it is, that the child shouldn't be behaving that way, how much they've had enough of this behaviour, how much this behaviour is effecting their life and their bond, and on and on in that direction.

Which parent do you think is feeling more stress? And why?

The answer is that Parent A would be feeling less stress because they are NOT in conflict with reality. The reality is that kids are probably going to tantrum at some stage in their little life (or a lot) because they are expressing their emotions in the only way they know how. They are learning how to deal with life's disappointments – not getting their own way all the time. This child's behaviour has nothing to do with the parent. It's about the child and what's happening for them.

Parent B on the other hand is in complete conflict with reality. The focus is on how this event shouldn't be happening, what effect this event is having on him/her and the judgements about that behaviour. None of which is in alignment with the reality of what is actually happening.

The child is having a tantrum. That's reality. Everything else is judgement, and judgement is debatable, depending on interpretation. Judgements are not true, factual reality.

Every day this week I will be teaching you how to become more aware of the specific thinking that lies behind your anger or your frustrations. The goal is to help you to change this thinking to be in alignment with reality and to alleviate stress.

HOW TO PUT TODAY'S LESSON INTO PRACTICE

Start taking notice of how your thoughts create your feelings. Recognise how you react to events that don't meet your expectations and become aware of your opinions/judgements on those events. Watch how your thinking escalates into more judgements and more 'proof' of your opinions being right.

Read more at ParentalStress.com.au

Follow us on Facebook:
facebook.com/parentalstresscentre

DAY 2
FIVE IMPORTANT TIPS FOR TAMING YOUR TEMPER

Today's lesson simply gives you five important tips that will arm you with tools for changing your thinking and avoiding angry outbursts.

1. All stress is a conflict between belief and reality.
It's never the events that cause stress. It's how we perceive these events. What you THINK about what you experience causes your emotions, not what your child is doing. When your thinking is in conflict with reality, you're usually thinking that something 'should' be different from what is actually going on. By bringing your thinking back into alignment with the reality of what IS happening, you will begin to decrease your stress.

THE REALITY IS IT HAPPENED and you can't change the past.

2. How do you know what to do until you learn what NOT to do?
Kids are learning and growing all the time. Think about how you learnt to run, walk, use a spoon etc. Did it happen overnight? No. It came with repetition and consistency (exactly why you are taking 28 days to tame your temper).

So when you are telling your child for the umpteenth time to do something, recognise that this repetition IS them learning how to do something, by learning the consequences of NOT doing it (just be sure they are tamed temper consequences).

3. Separate the human from the behaviour.

Your child's behaviour is simply a result of what they are thinking. It's not right or wrong - it's cause and effect. Rather than react to the behaviour, turn to understanding the thinking behind the behaviour instead. Why are they behaving this way? How do they perceive their life right now? How can you help them learn more about life, accept the current moment and/or teach them another way to behave?

4. You teach people how to treat you.

In any relationship there is a dynamic between the two of you. Both of you contributed to this dynamic by teaching each other what behaviour you will and won't accept. If your child is behaving in an unacceptable way, they are either trying out new behaviour to see if it works for them or it IS working for them because there is a payoff for them behaving in this way.

This may be because of how you have responded to this behaviour in the past (or NOT responded when you needed to). It's important to take a look at why they are behaving this way and what their payoff may be. You also need to look at how you may have contributed to the set-up of that behaviour through your role as a parent.

This understanding will help you to re-teach them how to treat you by starting to implement new strategies and consequences for this unacceptable behaviour.

5. Fight hate with love.

You can't fight with someone who is not fighting back. Make it a deliberate reaction to quiet your voice, get down to their level and have a mental picture of a time when they were at their most precious (sleeping or laughing perhaps).

Approach their behaviour with as much love and affection as you can muster. You might have to 'fake it 'til you make it', but you'll be surprised at the difference this makes on their behaviour, especially when combined with Tip Number 3 – separate the human from the behaviour.

You will find that these five tips will be expanded upon later as you progress through the challenge, but I wanted to begin with some 'food for thought' to get you started.

Remember to continue recognising your wins. This first week is likely to be the hardest. It always is when changing any habit, so hang in there.

By noticing ANY differences, you will start to see that change is possible. So notice those times where you did stop yourself from yelling, or when you changed your tone, or attempted to change your behaviour, because this is part of you making a conscious effort to change.

HOW TO PUT TODAY'S LESSON INTO PRACTICE

Write these five tips and a brief summary of each one on a piece of paper. Put it on your fridge to remind you of a different way to think about the challenging situations with your kids.

Read more at ParentalStress.com.au

Follow us on Facebook:
facebook.com/parentalstresscentre

DAY 3

TAKE AWAY YOUR JUDGEMENTS/LABELS AND WHAT ARE YOU LEFT WITH?

We're on day three now and things can be getting a bit wearing (if they weren't before now). This is probably due to your habits of judging the unwanted events of your daily life.

Here is a realisation I had that I recently shared on my Facebook page that will help you with this:

> *This morning after my shower, I came out to my kitchen and looked around.*
>
> *"What do you see?" I heard myself ask.*
>
> *"Mess" I replied.*
>
> *"No, that's your opinion of what you see. What do you actually see?"*
>
> *"Dishes to be washed, lunches to be made, juice spilt on the table I have to clean up, etc."*
>
> *"No, wrong again. That's your 'to do' list you think you see. What do you actually see?"*
>
> *"Ok, I get it. A sink, an oven, bench with food on it, dishes on a table, a light on. Actually, now I'm looking out the window and seeing a kookaburra sitting on the clothesline. The day is sunny, too."*

19

"What can you hear, touch or smell?"

"I hear the kids playing, the sounds of the birds outside, I can smell the freshness of today and feel a lot more peace having taken the labels off what I'm experiencing."

"This, my friend, is reality. Everything else is just judgement."

Take the labels and judgement off behaviour and just see it as behaviour. It is what it is. Yes, you need to do something about it in terms of teaching them it's not appropriate, but it doesn't have to be labelled as good or bad, right or wrong.

In fact, there is no good or bad, there's just cause and effect. The behaviour is just a result (the effect of what is happening for your child, which comes from their thinking).

Understand that without the judgements of right or wrong or any other labels you place on it (ADD, tantrum, naughty, stupid, silly, disrespectful, dirty, disgusting, etc.), you will begin to be a lot more productive about the problem, not to mention calmer.

Remember, it's your thoughts that get you cranky, not the behaviour itself. Strip the behaviour back to the five senses; what you see, hear, smell, touch or taste, and that is reality. Everything else is your judgement.

HOW TO PUT TODAY'S LESSON INTO PRACTICE

Become aware of when you are placing judgements on what is happening in your day and notice how they make you feel.

Deliberately take the judgement off the event by simply bringing your attention back to the five senses (what you see, what you hear, what you smell, what you touch, what you taste). Notice what a difference this makes to how you feel about this event.

Read more at ParentalStress.com.au

Follow us on Facebook:
facebook.com/parentalstresscentre

DAY 4
CHANGE THE PICTURE

How are you going with the challenge so far?

Usually, the first few days of change are either the easiest - because you become very deliberate about changing - or the hardest - because you have to be your most deliberate at stopping yourself.

The most fundamental part of being able to avoid anger is honing in on the concept that:

"All stress is a conflict between belief and reality."

I know it may seem like I'm harping on about this point, but that's only because it's really important for your progress towards controlling your anger (and subsequently your habit of yelling).

To get this concept at a deeper level, you need to become aware of exactly what beliefs are rolling around in your head that conflict with the current reality.

Yesterday you looked at the labels and judgements you placed on your reality. Today we want to look at the specific conversations you are having about your reality.

You see, stress/anger doesn't come from the events themselves. It comes from how you perceive each event and what you perceive it to mean about you or your life's self-worth.

Sometimes we begin with placing a label or judgement on an unwanted situation, but that can quickly escalate into that small event meaning your whole life is messed up.

Consider this: Here you are experiencing your child or children being defiant, unreasonable, upset, challenging or whatever may be happening for them. This is reality, however, this is what is going on in your head:

"Why did they do that? Why didn't they listen to what I said? They should be [insert correct behaviour here]. They shouldn't be [insert incorrect behaviour]. Why are they doing this TO ME all that time? I've had enough of them doing this to me all the time. Why can't they just leave me alone? I'm so over this happening in my life. I can't stand it anymore! I just want to run away! I hate my life!!!!"

While this is a dramatic end to this internal conversation for some, it may not be for others. I, for one, can relate to having had this conversation play out in my mind to this degree.

It all seems to begin with one tiny event, then a judgement about that event, then you begin rolling around in a story that is in conflict with reality. This quickly snowballs into what you now believe this situation means about you and your life.

What you think about expands in that direction. If you put your attention on how wrong a situation is, your brain will continue to seek out more evidence that you are correct and you'll find more and more wrong with your life. It will keep going in that direction until you are seething with anger because life isn't how it 'should' be (and look, I have the evidence to prove it).

Any thinking that is in conflict with your reality will cause you a degree of stress, depending on how long you allow this conflict to continue. So what you need to do is begin accepting the reality that is in front of you.

This event IS happening, regardless of your opinion of it. It's happening because of how everything unfolded in the past leading up to right now, and we cannot change the past.

What we can change, though, is the picture we have in our minds. Most of us often form pictures in our minds, an expectation of how we think something is going to occur.

When it doesn't happen that way, you need to let go of this vision as quickly as possible. Bring your attention back into alignment with what has ACTUALLY happened, so you can deal with it.

If you don't know how to deal with the reality of what is happening, educate and inform yourself from experts, other parents and resources that can teach you some ways to deal with the present behaviour.

I deliberately don't delve into 'how to' deal with the specific challenges with your children because there are already so many wonderful resources out there that teach this.

My focus is on teaching you how to deal with your mindset and how to accept your reality so that you can deal with these situations in a rational way. The skill of changing your thinking is a valuable one that is going to help you feel much calmer and in control of your emotions, because the reality is that you are going to come across a lot of challenging situations with your children.

HOW TO PUT TODAY'S
LESSON INTO PRACTICE

When I catch myself getting stressed over the kids (usually their fighting), the words that jolt me back to the current moment are, "You're in conflict with reality, Jackie."

This is usually enough to help me to CHANGE THE PICTURE in my mind.

Throughout your day, notice when you are starting to get angry and consciously bring your attention into the current moment. Look at what is actually happening. This is your reality right now. Let go of any thoughts/conversations about how something in the past shouldn't have happened or could have been different. Start looking at the reality of what is happening in this current moment.

Take notice of any regular patterns in your thoughts and/or how they quickly escalate into this little event meaning something about your entire life.

Read more at ParentalStress.com.au

Follow us on Facebook:
facebook.com/parentalstresscentre

DAY 5
IT'S ALL ABOUT ME

One of the most important things about understanding human behaviour is that we are all out to promote, improve or protect our perception of self-worth.

This is what drives ALL behaviour. How can I make myself feel better (or improve my quality of life)? How can I make myself feel worth more? How can I avoid pain? What's in it for me?

When dealing with your own behaviour, ask yourself:

- What do I think this 'unwanted' situation means about me?

- What is the judgement I'm placing on myself or my life because of this situation?

- Do I believe I'm a bad parent?

- Do I believe this event is evidence of me being stupid, useless or inadequate?

- Do I believe that this event is an interruption to my 'ideal' life?

- Do I believe this event means my life is going wrong?

Now question the reality of your answers.

If your best friend, or the person you love the most in the world, was experiencing this event, would you rate them or their life in the exact same way?

So if they are worthy in that same situation, why aren't you? If you believe they aren't worthy either in this same situation, question where this belief came from. Who dictated that worth was hinged on this situation being different?

Self-worth lies at the core of ALL stress, depression and anxiety, which is why I am so passionate about teaching parents an accurate view of self-worth - for you to feel better about yourself, but also so you can pass this knowledge onto your children.

Your perceptions of your self-worth are usually set up as a child through your experience of your parents and how you learnt to rate yourself in the context of life and family. Often these are incorrect perceptions of self-worth learnt from others who didn't know any better themselves.

Because you have learnt that self-worth is conditional and don't yet know that you are 100% worthy every moment of the day, there comes a need to continually promote, protect and improve your worth.

Anger is about power, trying to regain control of the situation. It fundamentally comes down to the belief that this event is compromising your self-worth in some way (or devaluing your life, even if it is just in a minor way).

Your reaction comes from the need to protect yourself from the pain of feeling worth-less (not worthless, but worth.....less) by defending it, trying to regain your power by being forceful with the intention of trying to feel 'better' – getting life back to the way you believe it needs to be in order to feel worthy again. This may not be the conscious thinking at the time, but it's the real reason why any of us get angry.

Here are some examples of this:

"This shouldn't be happening..." (because it's representing to me my inability to be a good parent or have a good life)

"They shouldn't be doing that..." (because they are interfering with my 'good life' or my abilities that I attach to my self-worth)

"I should've been able to......" (and that makes me feel worth-less somehow - stupid, useless, inadequate, a failure, etc.)

All of your initial thoughts about a situation will always come back to what you believe this situation means about your self-worth.

The shift in thinking comes once you realise that there is value in every moment - that not getting what you want provides you with information and learning for your personal development.

Your worth as a person comes, not by getting life to go your way, but because you are always learning and contributing to the unfolding of life (even when you aren't behaving in the most rational way).

Once you remember this, you stop needing to defend or protect your self-worth and you are left with the ability to allow life to unfold with ALL its ups and downs. All events are just experiences on your life's journey to be learnt from, not indications of your worth to the world.

If you are worth-less when life doesn't go to plan, then we are ALL worth-less, because ALL OF US experience adversities, hardships and challenges.

But we're not all worth-less. In fact, it's the complete opposite. Everyone is 100% worthy because we learn from our experiences, grow from them and contribute who we are to the rest of the world through our interactions with others. We become valuable contributors to other people's journeys and the lessons they learn.

In a nutshell, your worth comes from your existence, because you play a very important part in the unfolding of life.

You don't need to promote, improve, or protect your self-worth. You are already 100% worthy RIGHT NOW!

If you want more information on how to apply a new understanding of self-worth to your own life, all of my products teach you more about how to do this (especially in the context of being a parent).

Just go to www.ParentalStress.com.au to find out more about which product might suit your individual needs and budget.

HOW TO PUT TODAY'S LESSON INTO PRACTICE

Separate your self-worth from the event that's occurring. The reality is that we all experience ups and downs and they are not a reflection on your self-worth.

Instead, find the value in this event and the learning you are receiving from it to see that this is simply a part of your personal development.

Use this lesson in conjunction with the lesson three about taking the judgement off the event. Just deal with your present reality, without attaching any meaning to it about you or your parenting abilities.

Read more at ParentalStress.com.au

Follow us on Facebook:
facebook.com/parentalstresscentre

DAY 6
YOUR CHILD'S BEHAVIOUR IS NOT ABOUT YOU. IT'S ALL ABOUT THEM.

Yesterday you learnt a little bit about what drives your anger - the need to promote, protect or improve your perception of self-worth.

Well, this is happening for everyone else as well, including your children.

Try to detach from what you think your child's behaviour means about you (because it really doesn't mean anything about you) and start to look for what is going on for them.

What self-worth beliefs are driving their behaviour? If they're acting out, what's happening for them? Do they believe they are being hard done by? Do they feel like they are missing out on something? Do they feel criticised, judged, neglected, unloved, lonely, jealous, in need of attention? Or do they simply just want what they want because they want it?

Your child's feelings and behaviour will always be about their perception of the experience and what it means about them - their self-worth (and in a baby's case - self-preservation).

When you start looking at your child's behaviour with this desire to understand, you very quickly start to realise that their behaviour is not about you and what you want or need. It's all about them and what they want and need.

Their behaviour is not about what they are doing TO you. It's not about them trying to hurt you, disrespect you or make your life a living hell. It's about what they believe they want and need in their life to feel 'better' - to avoid their life from being worth-less.

Of course, that doesn't mean that their behaviour is okay, in some instances. However, with the understanding of what's driving their behaviour and the ability to detach it from meaning anything about you and your self-worth, you are then in a position to accept the reality of it (as opposed to being in conflict with reality - the cause of all stress).

Now you can begin dealing with your reality.

Now you begin dealing with the bigger picture - teaching your child life lessons about true self-worth, the reality of life's ups and downs, how to see the value in our unwanted events, how to understand emotions, the reality of cause and effect (if I behave this way, there are consequences), and so much more (this behaviour isn't tolerated in society, so it can't be tolerated in this context either; you make a mess, you clean it up; learning a skill comes with practice, etc.).

In essence, what you begin to do when you detach your self-worth from their behaviour is you begin dealing with the problem and focussing on its solution. This is much more productive than continually having to deal with your reaction to the problem, and quite often, consequently, their reaction to your reaction.

If you don't know how to deal with ongoing or habitual behaviour, there are millions of resources out there on techniques for dealing with challenging behaviour. Start resourcing solutions - websites, products, other parents, forums and friends to help you in the specific area in which you need help.

Once you stop rolling around in how wrong an event is and what it means about you, and instead, accept the reality that it is here (you don't have to like your reality, but you do need to accept it), then you can begin working on how to move forward from here.

Usually from this place, the 'unwanted' event comes and goes a lot quicker than when you are stuck in continual thoughts about how bad this unwanted event makes your life.

HOW TO PUT TODAY'S LESSON INTO PRACTICE

Detach your self-worth from the behaviour of your child. Look for what is happening in your child's mind to cause their behaviour. Look for what they may have their self-worth attached to so that you can give them a new understanding of life.

Keep in mind that this may not change their behaviour (they may not like their life lesson), however, keep reminding yourself that their reaction is not about you, but all about them.

Read more at ParentalStress.com.au

Follow us on Facebook:
facebook.com/parentalstresscentre

DAY 7
I FEEL LIKE I'M FAILING
THIS CHALLENGE DISMALLY

We're on day 7 now, and some of us have dropped the ball (including myself). It's harder than you think, isn't it?

I mean a 28-day tame your temper parenting challenge sounded all warm and fuzzy at the time, but now we're realising that it's A LOT harder than we thought, especially if it's a habit to yell.

Some of you may even feel like you are failing this challenge dismally...and that's what I want to address today.

I just googled the definition of failure and here's what it said: *"The condition or fact of not achieving the desired end or ends."*

So let me ask you, are you at the end of the challenge yet? Has it actually finished?

Many of you have read the title of this challenge as meaning you need to tame your temper for 28 days in order to be successful. However, what if the intention is really to be a parent with a tamed temper by the END of the 28 days? Then, it becomes a whole different story.

While you continue towards the 28-day mark, there are bound to be slip-ups. You are breaking a habit and that takes time. This is why we chose 28 days to begin with.

If you watched your toddler learning to walk, would you say that they had failed every time he/she fell down? Did you fail learning to walk, talk, or use a spoon? Or did it just take time to get the hang of it, stuffing it up lots of times along the way?

Well, think of this challenge the same way. You are learning to be a parent with a tamed temper and some of that journey will include you slipping back into old habits and then getting back onto the bike so you can keep going.

Don't give up now. The first week is always the hardest.

Revisit the tips I've given you so far.

All stress is a conflict between belief and reality.
What I am thinking vs what is actually happening.

How do you know what to do until you learn what NOT to do?
As I said above, part of learning is doing what you're trying not to do and taking notice of what caused it and what you can do differently next time.

Separate the human from the behaviour.
Try to understand the behaviour, where it comes from, what they're thinking. Don't attach the behaviour to any specific definition of your child.

You teach people how to treat you.
The way your children or others treat you is often part of a dynamic that you helped to set up. Have you always done everything for them? Have you accepted this behaviour before or possibly rewarded it somehow? Do they know that you will cave?

Fight hate with love.

You simply can't fight with someone who isn't fighting back. Eventually they will give up the fight when you stand your ground with love (that can still mean tough love distributed with compassion and affection).

Change the picture.

What did you expect that isn't happening? Remember these words: "You're in conflict with reality. Change the picture, because your expectations were not met. Right now is reality." Saying this to yourself when you notice you're getting annoyed will quickly pull your attention back into alignment with reality.

Take away your judgements and labels.

Srip it back to your experience (sight, sound, smell, taste and touch) - that's reality.

All behaviour comes back to self-worth - trying to promote, protect or maintain my perception of my self-worth (what's in it for me, how can I feel better, how can I avoid feeling worth-less). An insight into the self-worth component behind the behaviour can help you understand the behaviour a lot more. Then you can educate your children on how to feel better without the behaviour.

Whatever you do, don't give up. I know you can do this. I know I can do this, too (because I need that reminder as much as you do).

We all slip up, and sometimes we do it a lot before we get to the point where things change.

Nothing changes until something changes!!

Just continue to be aware of your thinking, your feelings and when/if you happen to yell. Just recognise it, learn about what was happening for you at the time and get back on the bike. Keep riding towards your goal of being a parent with a tamed temper by the end of your 28 days.

HOW TO PUT TODAY'S LESSON INTO PRACTICE

Keep going! It doesn't matter if you drop the ball. Just analyse what was happening for you that caused you to get angry and yell, by reflecting on the tips above. Think about what you might say to yourself next time an event similar to this arises.

Read more at ParentalStress.com.au

Follow us on Facebook:
facebook.com/parentalstresscentre

WEEK TWO:
The Shift to Reality

DAY 8
RECOGNISING YOUR WINS

Think about this challenge as if you were about to go abseiling down the highest cliff face in the world for the very first time.

When you look at how high up you are and how far down you have to go, it can be quite daunting, maybe a little bit scary (or a lot). "Can I really do this?" you may be asking yourself.

This is where you were at the beginning of the challenge.

As you take that first step, you are a little unsteady and really don't know which path you are going to take or where to put your feet next. However, your instructor is there to help you take each step and give you the information you need in order to take those first scary steps. You step off that cliff and you give it a go. You are shaky. You may even trip or freeze, but you keep going, learning more and more about the skill of abseiling and what it is you need to do in order to get down the cliff face.

This is what you've been doing in Week One of this challenge - learning about anger, what causes it and what steps you need to start taking to get you to your goal of being a parent with a tamed temper.

This week as you continue down the cliff face towards the finish line, we begin to look at the reality of being a parent and how changing your perspective on the challenges of parenting goes a very long way in relieving your angry reactions.

Before we begin to do this though, I think it's important to take some time to reflect on the week that was:

Grab a notebook and reflect over your week. Try to look at all the things you learnt over the week; about yourself, about your children and about what causes your anger.

Take some time to recognise the wins you've had and list them so that you can see that, even if you did drop the ball, this was an integral part of learning what you needed to move closer to your goal of being a parent with a tamed temper.

And while you're at it, why don't you begin writing a list of all the goals that you did achieve - the things you did manage to get done, in terms or your 'to do' list.

This is important, so don't glaze over this exercise. We spend too much time as mums and dads looking at what we're doing 'wrong' and not seeing all those successes we have.

DAY 9
FIND THE HIDDEN GOOD IN THE BAD

What you think about expands in that direction. You have one thought and then another thought and then it's like your attention particles begin one by one, to join in on the party. They continue to find more and more evidence of your initial thoughts being truth.

For example, let's consider the thought, "This is a crappy day." Your mind asks, "Why? Where's the evidence to validate this thought?"

"Well," you reply, "the kids woke up cranky and demanding at 5am. I had an awful sleep. Jordon threw a tantrum because he wanted his cereal, but he couldn't because there was no milk. Hayley was dilly-dallying this morning and made us late. Baby Ryan spewed all over my work clothes just as I was about to head out the door. My car was out of petrol which made us even later and I've just had enough of it all. Oh, and then there was the state of the house. It was completely messy, again. No one ever thinks to clean up after themselves. I have to do everything. I hate having to do everything. It's ridiculous. I shouldn't have to do everything. It really makes me angry when......blah, blah, blah."

And on and on it goes, continually finding more evidence of your crappy day and, meanwhile, the anger and resentment are growing.

Nothing changes until something changes.

So what do you think is going to happen if you continue to roll around in this story?

You will continue to feel as bad as you do.

But we live in a world of opposites. Where there is an up, there is a down. Where there is an in, there is an out. Where there is a reason to be sad, there is a reason to be happy. Where there is a bad event, there is a hidden good in there, too. The trick is to teach yourself to find it, and that is the learning for today.

Here is another Facebook status I posted that illustrates this point:

My baby isn't sleeping -
I'm missing out on my sleep. I'm a bad mum/dad. Why can't I do this?

<u>Or</u> *My baby is learning how to self-settle. I'm having an experience of parenthood in full force. I'm learning patience.*

My child is tantruming -
This is embarrassing. They should be listening to me. I should be able to stop them!
<u>Or</u> *I am teaching my child cause and effect. My child is learning about life and that they can't get their own way all the time.*

My partner and I are fighting –
My partner doesn't respect me, doesn't care about me. He's/she's an a**hole/b***h.

Or *We are learning a new dynamic and how to have a relationship as parents. This is just part of the ups and downs of relationships. We just need to understand each other's views and find a resolution.*

It's all a matter of perception. Today, make a conscious effort to find what the hidden good is in the bad parts of your day. Notice how you feel when you do this. Regular practice of this exercise will change the way you feel about your life, because you will begin to realise the value in ALL events, not just the ones that go to plan.

HOW TO PUT TODAY'S LESSON INTO PRACTICE

When things aren't going as expected, find the value in it. Do this for at least 5 unexpected events from your day.

Read more at ParentalStress.com.au

Follow us on Facebook:
facebook.com/parentalstresscentre

DAY 10
LOOK AT THE BIGGER PICTURE...
THIS TOO SHALL PASS

When we are experiencing something stressful, we often feel totally consumed by the moment. We are lost in our thoughts about this event and what we perceive it means about our lives (self-worth).

However, the bigger picture is that this event is just one event in the larger tapestry of your life. You will have many moments where you will experience unwanted events and many moments where you will experience wanted events.

All of the events you experience connect with each other. How did we get to this unwanted event? Well, because of all the experiences I had leading up to this current moment (the interactions I had with my kids, the decisions I made, the decisions my child made and other contributing factors).

If you look back enough, you will see that this event wouldn't have happened if something else hadn't happened, and then that event wouldn't have happened unless something else had happened. If you keep going back, you will see that ALL of your events are linked to the present moment in some way.

We need to keep this perspective when dealing with a current stressful event, but by looking to the future instead. This event is not the be all and end all of your life. It is simply one experience that will lead to many more experiences that make up your journey through life.

This event will come and it will go, and it will be replaced by more events - some wanted, some unwanted.

Ask yourself: Will this event matter to me this time next year? Has this event been here forever? Have any of my stressful events been permanent? Isn't it true that I have always experienced both highs and lows, and that this is simply one of those lows?

It's important to remember that EVERYTHING rises and passes away, everything!

When dealing with the challenges of parenting, remind yourself of this bigger picture and the connection that this event will have with better times, and more challenging times.

This is the reality of life and when you apply this reality, combined with yesterday's lesson to find the hidden good in the bad, there will be no resistance to ANY of your experiences. You will see that all events have value and all of them link together to make your unique journey through life.

'This too shall pass.' Maintain this perspective and nothing will faze you.

HOW TO PUT TODAY'S
LESSON INTO PRACTICE

*Widen back and look at situations that are causing
you stress in the context of the bigger picture of life.*

Read more at ParentalStress.com.au

Follow us on Facebook:
facebook.com/parentalstresscentre

DAY 11
AN EXERCISE TO HELP YOU LOOK AT THE 'BIGGER PICTURE'

In yesterday's lesson, I spoke about looking at the bigger picture by remembering that the reality of those challenging times with the kids is simply one event in the larger scale of your life, and that ALL events rise and pass away.

Today I wanted to give you an actual exercise to follow that will help you to expand your attention outside of the present stressful or consuming situation and, instead, look at it from a larger perspective.

This exercise can be especially helpful when dealing with things like the kids fighting, a tantrum, a crying baby or generally, when everything seems chaotic and you are feeling completely overwhelmed by it all.

The Expansion Exercise

Imagine you are an outsider looking down at you and your situation with your child.

Imagine what you would look like from this person's perspective, what your child would look like.

Now imagine looking down at the whole room that you are in.

How big are you now that you are looking at this whole room?

Now imagine looking down at your whole house and seeing yourself in that room.

How big are you now?

Now imagine that you are looking at yourself from above your whole street.

How big are you now?

Now imagine looking down at yourself from above your whole suburb, then your whole city, your whole state, etc. How big are you, as you keep expanding further and further?

Keep expanding your thinking until you FEEL how insignificant this moment is in comparison to the rest of the world (or universe if you get that far).

This little moment is only a small part of your life, of your whole existence, yet we easily get consumed by this small picture. Doing this visualisation helps to remind you that you are NOT what is happening right now. Life is so much bigger than this.

HOW TO PUT TODAY'S LESSON INTO PRACTICE

Follow the exercise above whenever you are feeling completely overwhelmed or about to explode.

Read more at ParentalStress.com.au

Follow us on Facebook:
facebook.com/parentalstresscentre

DAY 12
WHERE IS YOUR CHILD DEVELOPMENTALLY?

Raising kids is really tough. I don't think any parent would dispute that.

However, we need to keep stock of the reality of some specific words in the statement above, because we are '**raising kids**'. We are not raising adults.

Sure, they'll be adults one day and we have to prepare them for that, but becoming an adult takes time, lessons and physical growth in the brain and body - something that, quite simply, hasn't happened with your child at this stage of their development.

Yet, somehow we keep expecting them to think like adults, act like adults and rationalise like adults. We expect them to act in the same way that we would act with our 20, 30 or 40-something years of experience in this world.

This expectation that we have of them is in complete conflict with the reality of where they are physically and developmentally.

Whether you are expecting your baby to be able to sleep through the night, your toddler to be able to accept they can't have that toy at the shops, your kids to amicably solve arguments without fighting or yelling, or whether you are expecting your teenager to treat your advice with gratitude and regard you as a friend, not a foe; you are in denial with the truth of where they are in this stage of their life journey.

This conflict in thinking can lead us to getting frustrated with our kids when all we really need to do is remind ourselves that they are not adults yet. We cannot expect them to think and respond the way an adult would (or at least, how most adults with social etiquette would). We need to remind ourselves that they are still growing and learning.

Of course, we need to continue providing them with the lessons that they need in order to grow, develop and mature, but these lessons require repetition and consistency. We have to repeat these lessons over and over again before they have an effect - no different to learning how to walk, talk and use a spoon and no different to you applying the lessons from this challenge over and over again to create the habit of tamingyour temper.

Remembering this can go a long way to becoming more patient with the behaviour of our children.

HOW TO PUT TODAY'S LESSON INTO PRACTICE

Think about where your child is developmentally. Have they actually learnt what they need to in order to reach the expectations you have for them right now?

Take some time to do a little research into the brain development of your children (or the child that is challenging you). Educate yourself on what is physically happening in their brain at their particular age, so you can be more understanding of their behaviour and why they think the way they do.

Read more at ParentalStress.com.au

Follow us on Facebook:
facebook.com/parentalstresscentre

DAY 13
HAPPINESS MAY NOT ACTUALLY BE WHAT YOU WANT

"If the kids didn't do 'this', then I'd be a lot happier......"

"When the kids get a bit older, I'll be happier......."

"I can't wait for them to get through this stage........"

"If I could just get the housework done......."

So let me ask you, at what point do you actually become happy?

Well, today is about lifting the lid on this elusive goal of being happy.

The reality is that feeling happy is an emotion. Furthermore, it's an emotion we most often feel when life is going to plan. But the reality is - life doesn't always go to plan!

Tell me you are ever going to FEEL happy when you have 10 loads of washing to fold, a messy house, fighting/ whinging children and a million and one other things all campaigning for a piece of you at the same time.

You wouldn't FEEL happy if you lost a loved one, or lost your job, or got an unexpected bill you haven't budgeted for.

The emotion of happiness is not essentially what I believe we are all after, because most of us know that we won't always feel happy about all our life's experiences.

What I do believe we are after, though, is PEACE and that will come from being able to accept the reality of life's challenges and being able to find their value.

You don't have to like your reality, but you can be at peace with it by accepting your reality.

For example:

You won't like that you have lost a loved one, but you can be at peace with what they brought to your life while they were here. You can accept the reality that we all pass on at one time or another.

You may not like that you have 10 loads of washing to fold and a messy house, but you can be at peace with the reality that washing comes and washing goes, only to come back again, and that you will never reach the washing-free goal for long. A messy house gets cleaned and then it gets dirty again.

You may not like that your children are fighting, but you can accept the reality that kids will fight and that is part of them learning to get along.

It all depends on how you decide to look at it.

You can roll around in your story of how you think it shouldn't be happening or should be different, but at the end of the day, the current reality is what is actually in front of you.

You don't have to like it, but you do need to accept it. Accepting it is not saying "It's okay that it happened." It's more saying, "Should it have happened? No. But the reality is that it did, and I can't change the past. So what is the value in it and what am I going to do about it?"

Happiness will come and go as wanted events rise and give way to the unwanted. When you finally surrender to this reality and get into the habit of finding the value in ALL events, then you will be rewarded with a feeling of peace and contentment - that "I am at peace with my life exactly as it is, not just when it meets my ideals."

HOW TO PUT TODAY'S LESSON INTO PRACTICE

Become aware of when you are wishing life would be different to how it currently is and attaching your potential happiness to an outcome that hasn't arrived yet.

Instead of resisting what is currently happening, remind yourself of the reality of what is actually happening and look for how this current event is valuable. Remember, everything is linked, so there will either be something that this event is teaching you, some valuable information you are getting or something valuable that has come directly from this event.

Remind yourself that this event will rise and pass away just like others and is not attached to your overall happiness in life.

Read more at ParentalStress.com.au

Follow us on Facebook:
facebook.com/parentalstresscentre

DAY 14
PROBLEMS IN MY RELATIONSHIP CAUSE MY ANGER

Sometimes it's not even our child's behaviour that is the real issue that surrounds our anger. Often it can be a problem in our relationship, but it ends up being the kids who wear the brunt of our frustration.

The first piece of advice I would offer here would be to continue to remain aware of your thinking (which has been the theme throughout this whole challenge) and be honest with yourself about the source of your frustration.

When you observe the kids, being kids in their challenging way, practice bringing your attention back into the present moment. Instead of getting consumed by your thoughts about your relationship problem, ask yourself, "Where am I?" The answer will be: "Right here."

In that moment, there's nothing you can do about your relationship problem. All you have is right now and, in this moment, you are a parent who is dealing with what's happening in front of you. Make a conscious decision to think about the relationship problem at a later date.

When it does come time to think about the problem, sit down with a notebook and consider the events that have led up to these problems.

The reality of relationships is that you have two individuals who both hold their own unique belief systems, who are both getting new learning and information from their daily experiences, and who are constantly changing in accordance with the experiences they are having in life.

Because this is happening, there needs to be constant communication about how to integrate these changes within both of you to create alignment and harmony in your relationship.

In my book, *The Happy Mum Handbook*, I have dedicated an entire chapter to how you can begin to repair or maintain this alignment with each other.

But for the purposes of this lesson, start by being aware that the problem in your relationship has come from everything that has unfolded up to right now. This is reality. Where you are now in your relationship is where you are and you can't change the past. There's no point rolling around in how it 'should' be different, because the reality is that it's not different. It is how it is and you need to accept that before you can start dealing with it.

BOTH of you have contributed to setting up the current dynamic. You teach people how to treat you and both of you have contributed to teaching each other what you expect in a relationship, what your boundaries are, what you need, what you will and won't tolerate, etc.

Usually the relationship travels along relatively well until one person decides to change that dynamic without communication. The other one doesn't understand what is going on, because they are simply doing what they've always done, but you might be reacting differently and they don't get it.

This is why communication is paramount for re-discussing those boundaries, expectations and needs as they change. We all grow older, get wiser, change our goals and desires and, as a result, our ideals about our relationship change, too. We need to learn a way to communicate that with our partner to create alignment in the relationship.

But before you begin this communication, you first need to accept the reality of where you are and how you got there, considering how BOTH of you contributed to your current dynamic.

For example:

Perhaps you have never spoken to your partner about doing more around the house, or going out with friends and leaving you to do everything with the kids.

Your partner has learnt that you won't say anything and that there's no problem with continually doing this, because "He/she's got it covered and doesn't mind because he/she never says anything."

Meanwhile, you are silently resenting your partner's time away and all the work you need to do. Perhaps you're having little digs at them, but not making it clear that you are actually getting tired of this happening all the time and being left with the workload.

Then one day, you have finally had enough and lash out at the behaviour. Your partner has no idea where this has even come from and just jumps into defensive mode, feeling unjustifiably attacked. Then the argument begins. You try to communicate that he/she is wrong and you are right, and your partner does the same. No one is listening to each other. No one is acknowledging the reality of how both of you contributed to the current problem and, hence, no resolutions are being sought. You just continue to go back and forth playing the right and wrong game.

Feelings then escalate. You're both consumed by thoughts of how it 'should' be different and how 'wrong' the other person is, which causes you to feel angry. The kids play up and the screaming begins.

There is another way, though, and the first steps are to consider how this problem was set up and to acknowledge the reality of where you are right now. Talk to your partner about what you both believe the solution is and negotiate a resolution where both of you get part of what you want.

HOW TO PUT TODAY'S
LESSON INTO PRACTICE

Practice staying in the present when dealing with your children. Get out of your head and your thoughts about the relationship problem. Consciously allocate a specific time for you to sit down, and either consider the problem yourself first or create a time to chat with your partner about the problem.

Deliberately consider how you've both contributed to the current way you both behave towards each other and consider what you would like to happen. Decide what you are willing to compromise on and stay solution-focussed.

Don't fall back into how it 'should' be. Stay focussed on reality and how to move forward with a solution that works for both of you.

Read more at ParentalStress.com.au

Follow us on Facebook:
facebook.com/parentalstresscentre

WEEK THREE:

Let's Get
Solution-Focussed!

DAY 15
STOP!
WHAT IS SO IMPORTANT ABOUT THIS ANYWAY?

There are two things that I've noticed about my own impatience during this challenge. The first is my incessant need for everything to be done when I want it done, and secondly, how attached I get to achieving what I'd set out to do, without ANY interruptions whatsoever. If I can't achieve these two things, I can feel myself getting all riled up.

I'm guessing you can see the potential conflict with reality within these two expectations.

Firstly, there is no such thing as a fast-moving child (unless, of course, it involves chocolate and red cordial), so the expectation that things will be done in my time is unlikely - at least not every time.

The reality is that children aren't able to do things as fast as me sometimes - either because of a lack of co-ordination, a lack of knowledge about what they're doing, or quite simply because they lack the understanding of why they actually need to hurry in the first place.

So I really need to remind myself of this reality so I don't get so impatient and lose my cool.

Secondly, let's take a look at this whole attachment we seem to have to achieving our expectations. When you set goals - for example, to clean up the house, cook dinner or go grocery shopping - what is it that we get so worked up about when it doesn't go to plan?

Consider this for a minute: What are you going to do when you get the goal? What then?

Okay, so I get my house clean, what's going to happen then?

Umm, it gets dirty again and I will then clean it again.

What are you going to do when you cook dinner?

You'll eat it, do the dishes, then go on to do other things. Tomorrow you will do the same.

What will happen when you get to the shops?

You'll buy the groceries, put them in your car, go home, put them away and then move on to your next goal.

The point is that when you get the goal or achieve what you set out to do, you are just going to set another goal and do something else. We never stop setting goals. Life goes on and next week you won't even think about the fact that last week you didn't get dinner ready on time or that you ran 5 minutes late to work.

So the question to ask yourself is:

What is so important about this anyway?

Because the value in life is not even about achieving. Achievement is not the real purpose of a goal. The true purpose of setting goals is that when we set them, we are setting life in motion. Setting goals makes us DO life. When we set a goal, we make plans, have experiences, meet and interact with people and we learn lessons about life.

Bottom line is: We learn, grow and have experiences on the way to the goal, when we get the goal and when we don't get the goal.

The best way to learn to let go of your attachment to outcome is to recognise that achieving what you set out to do is not the important part of life. It's all the stuff that happens in between.

Don't fall into the trap of all life's pleasures being pinned on that short-lived feeling of joy you experience when you actually achieve a goal. The reality is that you will experience very few moments of joy in your life because we don't always get what we want.

Instead, try to find the joy in all of those little bits in between, where you can choose to actually experience the joy OF LIFE.

You know, those times where your child was laughing, playing, enjoying the moment, asking you for a cuddle, or to read a story, or to 'help' you - all of those things that happen WHILE you are getting to the goal of cooking dinner, for example.

These are the moments that are important.

At the end of your days, when you look back at your life, old and frail, what do you think will end up being the important bits of your life? Do you think it will be just about the times where you achieved what you set out to do? Or will it be just as much about those precious, priceless moments in between that made up the best parts of your life?

HOW TO PUT TODAY'S LESSON INTO PRACTICE

Become aware of those times when you notice yourself holding on too tightly to a particular outcome, goal or achievement you are trying to reach.

ASK YOURSELF:
What is so important about this anyway?

Take some time to recognise the value in the current events leading up to achieving your goal. What are you learning? What are you experiencing right now? How is this valuable? Or what can you enjoy about this current moment?

ASK YOURSELF:
When I'm old and frail looking back on my life, what would I consider important from these moments surrounding this event?

Do this and you'll be looking at your goals from a very different perspective.

Read more at ParentalStress.com.au

Follow us on Facebook:
facebook.com/parentalstresscentre

DAY 16
LET'S GET SOLUTION-FOCUSSED!!

As I've mentioned many times throughout this challenge, all stress is a conflict between belief and reality.

These last two weeks I have been progressively teaching you how to understand the specific beliefs (thinking) behind your anger/stress and how to change your thinking to be in alignment with reality.

Now we begin to move on to the next phase of our challenge - solutions. Just because we accept our reality (i.e. reality is what I'm currently experience and that is due to the unfolding of everything that happened leading up to now - none of which I can change), doesn't mean we will like our reality.

It also doesn't mean that we won't want to change our reality. So this week I am going to teach you how to apply and resource solutions to the issues we are experiencing with our children.

Before you do this though, you need to first get very clear about what it is you actually want.

We often spend so much time thinking about how bad or wrong our life is, but we don't actually turn our attention to what we want to happen in our life. We are too busy looking for all the things we are missing out on.

For example, rather than seeing how little time you have for yourself, consider how much time out you would like and what you would like to do when having your time-out. What hobbies or favourite past times would you like to pursue? Would you like some time to yourself once a week, a coffee with a friend, a couple of nights off cooking, a weekly drink or two with the boys (if you're a dad)?

What is it that you want that would provide the solution to this problem you are having?

If it is a problem with your child and a 'stage' they are going through, what is it that you expect from them and by when?

Accepting reality doesn't mean you have to just put up with the unwanted situations in life. The value in receiving unwanted events is being able to learn from them and setting goals to keep our life moving forward.

Later in the week we are going to look more at potential solutions to your problems, but for today I'd like you to simply catch yourself thinking about what you're missing out on or rating something as 'wrong'.

Think about what you DO want that could stop you from missing out or consider what might be the RIGHT way instead of the wrong way and whether that could be your potential goal.

Consider whether these opposites may just be goals that are worth setting for yourself, or whether perhaps you are in conflict with reality again.

For example, let's say you caught yourself saying "I never get any time to myself." What's the flip side to this? How much time would you like to yourself? (Be realistic now - a month's holiday probably isn't feasible.)

Or another example is let's say you caught yourself saying "I don't want to get up to this child again. I've had enough." The flip side to that may be, "Okay, so I won't get up to my child." But is this realistic? The reality is that you probably will have to get up to your child, however, perhaps the solution is that you find some time to take a break, catch up on some sleep or take turns with your partner at getting up.

So recognise, yet again, what you are thinking about, catch those thoughts and turn them around to try and list some solutions to your current issues.

HOW TO PUT TODAY'S LESSON INTO PRACTICE

Grab a notebook and keep it near you for the next few days. Create two columns in the notebook - one side says "The problem is........."; the other side says "The solution might be......" Consider how realistic the potential solution is and whether it may be a potential goal for you to pursue.

As mentioned, we will do more with this list as we proceed through the challenge. This exercise is just about gathering information on current issues and considering potential solutions.

Read more at ParentalStress.com.au

Follow us on Facebook:
facebook.com/parentalstresscentre

DAY 17
FIVE 'IN THE MOMENT' TIPS FOR AVOIDING ANGER

Before we move on to looking for the long term solutions, I wanted to spend today and the next couple of days giving you some 'in the moment' solutions for avoiding angry outbursts. Let's face it, these outbursts only end up in us feeling guilty, the kids crying or acting out, and an increased level of self-criticism for dropping the ball.....again.

Here are some ways to avoid all that and keep your cool:

1. Get Yourself a PAUSE Button

Select something that you can wear to remind you of your mission to avoid anger. A rubber band that you can flick on your wrist to bring your attention back to reality can help. A hair tie will do the same thing. A special bracelet (for the ladies) that moves up and down your arm can serve as a reminder, or even a necklace that you can play with often. These can all be useful to serve as your PAUSE button.

Whenever you experience yourself tensing or when you recognise your thoughts are getting away from reality (what's in front of you), start playing with your PAUSE BUTTON. This will remind you to bring your awareness back into the current moment and the reality of what is actually happening.

2. Sing Out Your Frustrations

This is one of my favourite tools for avoiding anger. There are two ways you can do this:

a) Use the melody of your favourite song, and instead of singing the real words, sing out what you really want to say and what you are frustrated about, or make up your own melody and sing out your frustrations.

OR

b) Choose a song that you absolutely love or that calms you down and sing it to the very best of your ability. Pretend you are auditioning for The Voice or a talent show. Your attention will be so focussed on your singing ability you will forget to be angry. My favourite song to sing (although it's not my actual favourite song) is Amazing Grace. I find that my anger, and often my kids' anger, usually calms down by singing this one.

3. Consciously Experience Your Anger

Resistance is persistence! Whatever you resist ends up lasting longer. The same will apply to your feelings. We know that everything rises and passes away, but before your feelings can pass away, they need to be experienced or expressed. Otherwise, where does the energy go?

Often, once we begin to feel angry, we resist the urge to express it. Instead we silently seethe while continuing the same line of thinking that's in resistance with what is actually happening (in conflict with reality). Consequently, the feeling of anger increases.

Eventually, needing somewhere to go, this feeling of resistance ends in us yelling or throwing something (this used to be the two ways I would experience it).

Instead of putting yourself through all that, simply acknowledge how you feel and actually feel your anger exactly as it is, without judgement. What exactly is this feeling inside me that I label as anger? Where does this feeling sit in my body? Where are its edges? Where does it start? Where does it stop? How far out does it expand? What does it even FEEL LIKE to be angry?

When you consciously experience this feeling of anger, you allow it to be there. The reality is that this feeling is not right or wrong, it's about cause and effect. There are thoughts that cause stress and there are thoughts that don't cause stress. All that has happened here is that you have had thoughts that have caused you stress and you are now experiencing the physical results of those thoughts.

You can't change the past and what you are experiencing is the present reality of past thoughts - SO EXPERIENCE IT. Allow it to be there without judging it, just feel it and watch it rise and pass away.

Stop what you are doing for a minute and really feel what it feels like to be angry in your body and let it be. Stop resisting it and accept the experience of it. This is your reality right now.

You will be surprised at how powerful this tip is.

4. Imagination and Visualisation

Imagine or remember your child at a time when they were being sweet, lovable, precious, funny or cute. Usually, picturing them smiling is helpful, or when they are asleep and all innocent-looking.

This will help you to remember that they are not the behaviour they are currently exhibiting. They are much more than that. This is just them behaving a certain way because of how they've perceived their life right now, and what they believe it means about their self-worth (remember the self-worth lessons?).

5. Change the Ambience in the Home
There are a few ways that you could do this:

a) Say to the kids: "Okay, stop. Everyone stop for a minute! I've decided we are going to have a happy day today. We are no longer going to be grumpy or whinging. We are going to start our day over and bring out our happy side. We're going to get back into our beds and get back out again, ready for our happy day." Take them back to their rooms. You do the same. Literally get back into bed and back out of it again. Make a game of it. It will shift their moods and they'll find it funny.

b) Put on some music and jump around all silly-like. Dance on the coffee table, bounce on the couch, throw yourself around like you did at a teenage dance party. Change the atmosphere with a bit of silliness and fun. Pick some music that you find energising and just go for it. Not only will the kids love it, you will also be releasing that pent up energy that originally had nowhere to go but out of your mouth in the form of yelling. Dads, get out your rock songs and bring out the air guitar!

c) Go outside. Our problems end up seeming so much smaller when we are experiencing them outside (especially when you are listening to crying, whinging or fighting children).

HOW TO PUT TODAY'S LESSON INTO PRACTICE

Follow any one of these tips when those overwhelming feelings of anger start to arise.

Read more at ParentalStress.com.au

Follow us on Facebook:
facebook.com/parentalstresscentre

DAY 18
ALL YOU HAVE TO DO IS SURRENDER

Yesterday, one of my tips was to consciously experience your anger. That idea comes from the technique of mindfulness - being in the present moment without judgement.

Five years ago I attended a meditation retreat called Vipassana. It was a retreat where you meditated in silence for 10 hours a day for 10 days. You weren't allowed to speak with anyone, contact your family, read or listen to music. I was just left with me and my mind.

There are a few things that this meditation course taught me, and the first of those was the realisation that everything rises and passes away eventually. Everything is impermanent.

This lesson was learnt by focussing on the sensations that occurred in the body without judgement over those 10 days. By doing this, I experientially felt the rising and passing of sensations that came from emotions, pain (we had to sit without moving for an hour everyday towards the end), itching and other random tingles that would come and go.

By consciously allowing yourself to feel and experience your anger, you are allowing it to rise and pass away quicker, because you are not holding onto it with resistance.

Today I want to take you through another form of 'in the moment' meditation that will help you reconnect with the 'bigger picture' and avoid the habit of getting consumed by anger.

I do this exercise quite a bit when the kids are running amok and, because you don't necessarily have to close your eyes, it can be pretty much done anywhere at any time.

All you have to do is begin by breathing in through the nose and out through the nose and connect with what it feels like to have the air going in and the air going out.

Feel what it feels like as your body responds to this air going in and air going out. Feel the rise and fall of your body's reaction to the air going in and out, and notice how it responds to the air, regardless of any control you have or your opinion of it.

Keep focussing your attention on your breath going in and out and the flow of your body responding as it needs to. Whenever you notice your attention wandering, just gently bring it back without judgement to the air going in through the nose and out through the nose and how it feels in the body to do that.

Just go with the flow of that breathing for a while and notice how peaceful you feel when you surrender to the flow of the breath.

Now make the connection between the rise and fall of the body with the reality of life. Everything in life rises and passes away. Events come in and events go out, regardless of your opinion of it, regardless of your control, just like we breathe. When you allow yourself to experience the flow of this reality without judgement, and allow yourself to surrender to the flow of life's ups and downs, you feel more peace.

Keep focussing on your breathing, the flow of it, the body's rise and fall in response to the air going in and the air going out and how this is an analogy of life's events, too.

Reconnecting with this feeling when something is not going to plan and is causing you to feel stressed can reduce your reactions and help you stay calmer. I often have to use this technique when I'm grocery shopping with my two boys. They seem to just run amok - laughing, talking loudly, running, wrestling, pushing the trolley into people accidentally, etc.

I have to just allow myself to go with the flow of this moment and reconnect to the knowledge that it will rise and pass away. Also, I can't control their behaviour (although I still try with the usual threats, punishments, etc.), so I need to just surrender to the flow of the event coming in, knowing that it will leave again soon enough.

HOW TO PUT TODAY'S
LESSON INTO PRACTICE

Whenever you are experiencing an overwhelming event that you can't seem to change, the only way to get through it without feeling stressed is to surrender to it.

Follow the instructions above to bring yourself back into experiencing the reality of life's ups and downs. Connect to the rise and fall of your breath responding to the air going in and the air going out.

Notice how your body responds to the air, regardless of your opinion of it and regardless of your ability to control. It just happens. When you allow these uncontrollable events to 'just happen' and surrender to it, you will feel peace.

Read more at ParentalStress.com.au

Follow us on Facebook:
facebook.com/parentalstresscentre

DAY 19
ANGER MANAGEMENT BY SELF-CARE

What makes this challenge different from anything else is that you are no longer trying to control the external events (e.g. your child's behaviour) to stop your anger.

It is my intention to educate you on how to empower yourself to tame your temper, rather than rely on somebody else to behave in a certain way before that can happen.

So far we've been focussing more specifically on your mindset, but in this lesson I want to highlight other things you can do that will support a healthy mind so that it will be a little easier to think in alignment with reality.

You can do this by focussing on caring for yourself. Here are four ways in which you can do this:

1. Take care of your physical self

The other day I finally pulled my finger out and did some exercise. I turned on the Nintendo Wii and put on Just Dance 3 and danced my little heart out for an hour (with the kids by my side doing it, too). When I finished, I thought to myself, "Why don't I do that more often? I feel fantastic!"

We all know the benefits of exercising for the body. Strangely enough, it gives you more energy, it's great for the muscles, for your metabolism and, consequently, for weight loss, etc. I don't need to tell you about all that again. But why don't we do it?

It's the same again with food. Most of us know how to eat healthy, but those bad foods just keep getting put in our mouth.

If you want to support the challenge to tame your temper, then eating well and exercising will go a long way towards achieving this. When the body is under stress, you are feeling tired or listless and feeling all icky and unhealthy. It becomes harder to have the mental strength to deal with life's challenges, too.

2. Be mindful of what you wear.

If you are feeling low, wear something nice. Make the effort to get yourself dressed for the day. Mums, apply a bit of make-up, make some time to do your hair (sure you may have to get up 5-10 minutes earlier, by hey, you're worth it). Dads, put on a nice shirt, maybe comb your hair. Put a bit of pride into how you look. You will feel much better about yourself when you are giving yourself the time to 'pretty yourself up'.

Also, be aware of how your clothes can affect your body's ability to function correctly. I remember when my kids were toddlers, I had a pair of pants that I would wear that were a little bit too small (my hips had widened from childbirth). I was in complete denial about them being too small and wore them anyway. They must've been squashing my hips because I began to notice that every time I wore them, I would feel quite irritable. This is because my body was under pressure to function properly in these pants, so eventually, I needed to get rid of them.

The same sort of thing can happen if you are wearing clothes that don't warm you up enough, or clothes that make you too hot and sweaty. For you mums - even wearing a bra that's too tight or not supportive enough can have an effect on your back, your neck, and even give you headaches. For dads, tight underwear can have the same effect (or so my husband tells me). These things can cause pressure on your body and, hence, your mood.

3. Meditate.

As mentioned in yesterday's lesson, I have experienced the huge benefits of meditation, and although I am guilty too of not allowing specific time to meditate on a daily basis, I know that when I really need it, it makes such a wonderful difference to my life.

4. Love your body exactly as it is.

We pay too much attention to the parts of ourselves that make us insecure. Most of those parts can't even be changed (at least not without expensive and risky surgery). So instead of hating on yourself all the time, let's try focussing on what IS working within our body and appreciate that.

Here's a little exercise on how to do this:

When you have a shower/bath next, start at the top of your head and, working downwards, begin lovingly and gently caressing each part of the body. Take notice of all the areas of your body you appreciate and/or like.

Notice what parts of the body are serving you well - your brain, your hearing, your eyes, your legs, your chest (especially for mums who are or have breastfed), and your arms. What attributes do you like about yourself?

Continue caressing and stroking, caring for your body and appreciating all of those unique things that make up you and allow you to experience your life. Go all the way down to your toes.

This little exercise when done regularly helps you to accept yourself just the way you are and reminds you that there are so many parts of you that are fabulous and that help you to function from day to day. There is so much to appreciate about you. You just need to look for it.

HOW TO PUT TODAY'S LESSON INTO PRACTICE

Bottom line is: TAKE CARE OF YOU.

When you take care of you, you teach others that you are worthy of being cared for, you function better, you think clearer and you, consequently, handle life's challenges better.

Make some time for yourself to exercise, eat well, dress comfortably, meditate and love yourself exactly as you are right now.

While you may not have time for all of these things every day, make it a priority to do at least one of these things on a daily basis.

Your body and mind will thank you for it.

Read more at ParentalStress.com.au

Follow us on Facebook:
facebook.com/parentalstresscentre

DAY 20
KNOWLEDGE IS POWER –
HOW TO GET WHAT YOU WANT

On Day 16 I mentioned the common tendency a lot of us have to focus on what you are NOT getting, as opposed to what you WANT.

I suggested that over the next few days you should begin looking at the ideal of the situation and what the solution might be to the problem you are experiencing.

Just because we accept the reality of what is happening, that doesn't mean we won't want to change our reality. So in today's lesson, we're going to look at exactly HOW you can change that reality.

Once you've established what it is that you want or the ideal of the situation, the next step is to think about HOW TO GET WHAT YOU WANT or reach that ideal.

Where can you get the information on how to work towards your goals?

How do you even begin teaching your kids how to behave appropriately and stop those tantrums or backchat, or to treat you with respect?

How do you begin to improve your marital relationship or change your financial situation?

Well, it all begins with looking for the information. The beauty of today's world is that we are surrounded with an abundance of resources that will educate us on how to get what we want. So start using these resources. Knowledge is power!

Start looking for the information you need from parenting forums, books, internet, friends, family, other parents, experts in this field, support groups, etc.

Look for people who have been through what you are currently going through. Find out how they've handled it, what tips they have and how they got through it.

The reason why we are all valuable is because we exist. Each of our existences contributes knowledge and information to those around us because of what we have experienced and learnt ourselves. So use other people's information to help yourself. Don't be ashamed by what you don't know. Accept the reality that we DON'T know everything. Don't assume that just because you are a parent you should automatically know everything there is to know about raising children. We are all learning and growing and we need each other to learn how to 'do' life differently or progress through our challenges.

When you focus your attention on finding solutions to a potential problem, you begin finding resources that will teach you how to reach your goals.

But you have to start by consciously focussing your attention on getting the information and learning what you need to progress through your problem and towards your desired outcome.

HOW TO PUT TODAY'S LESSON INTO PRACTICE

Think about what you want and start searching for the information you need to learn how to get what you want.

ASK YOURSELF:

What is the ideal solution to this problem?
What information do I need to learn in order to get to my ideal solution?
Who might already have the information I need to teach me how to solve this problem?
Where can I begin to get this information?

REMIND YOURSELF:

There's nothing wrong with me for not already knowing this information.
I am a learning human being who doesn't know everything about everything.
If I knew how to fix this already, I would've done it, so clearly I need more information.
It's okay to learn off others and ask for help.

Read more at ParentalStress.com.au

Follow us on Facebook:
facebook.com/parentalstresscentre

DAY 21
JUST TAKE TIME OUT!
YEAH, WHY DON'T I JUST DO THAT?

"Mums and dads need to take time out for themselves."

This is what we are endlessly told as parents. We know this advice well. We even know that we should probably follow that advice, and we often mean to, but somewhere in there, we just seem to fall by the wayside in favour of everyone else's needs.

Often, we believe that we don't have enough time to take any personal time out.

However, having the time to do something is not about time, it's about PRIORITIES!

Think about it. Have you ever had a whole string of things that you planned to do in a specific timeframe, yet a friend happens to call you, devastated by a sudden breakup or upheaval at work, and you want to be there for them? You end up speaking to your friend for an hour and get hardly anything done on your list by the expected time.

Was the choice to talk to your friend about time? Or did you MAKE time in your schedule for your friend because IN THAT MOMENT it became your priority over getting your list done?

So do you really not have time to do some things for yourself? Or do you just keep making other things a priority?

As mentioned in Day 5, there is always a self-worth component behind all of the choices we make and actions we take. Your priorities will always be about which decision is going to improve, promote or protect our self-worth (i.e. make me feel 'better').

There is a reason why you don't have time for yourself, and it's not about time. It's about your priorities in each moment and how you believe this is going to make you feel.

For example, let's take the choice of ironing and cleaning up the house when the kids go to bed or reading a book and relaxing.

Ironing and cleaning will mean that I will get it all done without interruption, will feel organised in the morning and feel good about myself to know I've got it all done. I will be fulfilling my role as a good parent and my identity of being a clean and organised person.

On the flip side, I could read a book and relax and that will make me feel pretty good, but I just know that the mess will drive me crazy. I'll end up feeling frustrated that I have to do it later, so I might as well do it now.

Neither choice is right or wrong. It just comes down to your priority in that moment. The priority that holds the greater weight for making you feel better will be the one that wins out.

So, in fact, you weren't actually putting others before you. You were actually working in the best interests of yourself 100% of the time. This is the reality of all human behaviour.

Here's another example:

I could organise for my parents/a friend/a relative to look after my children once a month so that my partner and I can have a night out together. That would make me feel good. However, I also believe that my children are my responsibility and I shouldn't just palm them off for someone else to look after. That would make me feel like I wasn't being a very good parent.

Two conflicting beliefs. Only one can win out. Whichever belief is going to make you feel the most worthy will always win out. Hence the choice in that moment would probably be to stay home and look after your children and miss out on the night out once a month.

Again, not right or wrong, just about beliefs and priorities.

HOW TO PUT TODAY'S LESSON INTO PRACTICE

We all know that taking time out from your parenting responsibilities can be important for keeping you sane and calm with a tamed temper. If you aren't doing that for yourself, but you'd like to, consider why you aren't making it a priority already.

What is your pay-off for choosing the other activity over what you'd like to do? How will the other activity make you feel 'better' as a person, give you a 'better' life or improve, promote or maintain your perceived self-worth? Notice how that priority holds more weight over taking that time for yourself.

Recognise that whatever decision you are making, this IS you making yourself a priority. (e.g. even giving to charity makes you feel like a good person, or always give to my children first, so I can feel like I'm being a good parent)

Realising why you prioritise one thing over another may just help you to change how you decide to spend your time, or it will at least give you the understanding that you ARE making a choice to do something that serves you.

Read more at ParentalStress.com.au

Follow us on Facebook:
facebook.com/parentalstresscentre

WEEK FOUR:

The Continual Road to Successful Tame Your Temper Parenting

DAY 22

THE ROAD TO SUCCESSFUL TAME YOUR TEMPER PARENTING

You are about to enter into the final week of the Tame Your Temper Challenge and, hopefully, you are finding it just that little bit easier than week one.

This week I wanted to introduce you to my five-step process that will help you tame your temper and enable you to handle any challenge that comes up in parenthood and in life. It's a process I use in my book, *The Happy Mum Handbook*, in my 12 week online *Postpartum Depression Recovery Program* and in my 4-part webinar series: *How to End Parenthood Stress and Depression*. It's also one that I use all the time in my own life.

It's called my Mind TRACK to Happiness Process.

The word TRACK is an acronym for the five steps of the process, making it easier for you to remember and apply. You won't have to keep checking what you need to do in stressful situations.

I know myself, from doing a lot of personal development stuff that you walk away from having read new information feeling very inspired and motivated to change, only to find that a week later you are right back where you started from.

The Mind TRACK to Happiness Process will help keep you on track with your tamed temper parenting by helping you to remember your thoughts and to stay solution-focussed.

Incidentally, this five-step process pretty much sums up all that you have been learning over the past three weeks. Here is what each letter stands for:

> T – Thoughts
>
> R – Reality
>
> A – Aim
>
> C – Choices
>
> K – Know Your Plan & Action It

The first step is THOUGHTS – recognise what you are thinking about the situation you are experiencing. We have been focussing a lot on this during the challenge, because all stress is a conflict between belief (what I'm thinking) and reality (what is actually happening or an accurate perspective of what is happening). However, you can't change what you don't acknowledge, so the first step is to become aware of your thinking.

The next step of the process is REALITY. Once you recognise your thoughts, you need to align them with the reality of the current moment, the reality of what is happening and the reality of what it really means to be experiencing what you are (learning, development, part of life's ups and downs, it's not about my self-worth or success in life, etc.).

The third step is AIM. Now that you have accepted the reality of your present moment, you want to move on to the solution to your problem by asking yourself – What do I want? There's also a couple of other questions to ask to test your aim, making sure that it's realistic and in alignment with reality. (For example, check you aren't setting aims to make your child's behaviour perfect every time.)

The fourth step is CHOICES. What choices, solutions and resources are available to teach me what I need to know to get me closer to the AIM that I set in Step Three? This step is about educating yourself by searching for HOW to get what you want.

The final step is KNOW YOUR PLAN & ACTION IT. Once you have established what you want, you now need to put it into practice. From the information that you gathered in Step Four, you can decide on what your plan of attack is to start moving towards your aim, and begin to actually take those steps.

Over this week I will go into each step in more detail, giving you a few more tips and examples on how to implement this process into your own life. You can also use it as a summary of everything that you've learnt in this challenge.

I want you to be armed with everything you need to start making some permanent changes to your life so that you don't let go of the new habits you've been learning, including taming your temper. I'm sure you've seen the benefits this challenge has had on your family and yourself (I know I have), so this week is about learning how to keep it going this way.

HOW TO PUT TODAY'S LESSON INTO PRACTICE

From what you have learnt so far from this challenge, get into the practice of following the five steps of the TRACK process.

If it helps, write down the five steps on some paper and put it where you will see it often to remind you of how to do it.

T – Thoughts

R – Reality

A – Aim

C – Choices

K – Know Your Plan & Action It.

Read more at ParentalStress.com.au

Follow us on Facebook:
facebook.com/parentalstresscentre

DAY 23
WHAT AM I THINKING?
STEP 1 OF THE MIND TRACK TO HAPPINESS PROCESS

The primary thinking that underlies all anger is the belief that the event that you are experiencing 'should' be different.

You have an expectation in your mind of how the event should've gone, yet what you are experiencing is entirely different.

However, the change in the event – the unwanted event - is not what is causing you to be angry. It is your thinking, which is stuck in conflict with the reality of the new 'unwanted' event.

In the first step of the Mind TRACK to Happiness Process, before you can stop the anger, you must first recognise the thinking that is causing the anger.

"This shouldn't be happening."

"They 'should' be doing something different."

"I should be doing something different."

"I shouldn't have to deal with what's going on in my life."

"Why can't I just........?"

All of these kinds of thoughts roll around in your mind, gaining momentum and causing the physical sensation in your body that we label as anger.

On a deeper level, not only are you getting angry over the difference between what you expect and what has happened, you are also attaching that event to what you believe it means about your life.

"I've had enough of dealing with this IN MY LIFE."

"There it is again, evidence of me being a HOPELESS PARENT."

"Why can't I BE LEFT ALONE for just five minutes? Why do they always BUG ME!? Why do I HAVE TO DO everything?"

"I just feel so USELESS / HELPLESS."

"Why is he/she doing this TO ME?"

All of the above statements are concluding how you or your life has been devalued in some way. This leads to an increase in the angry reaction within your body.

The thinking that lies behind anger is ALWAYS in conflict with reality – the reality of the actual event that is occurring and the reality of true self-worth.

The THOUGHTS step on the TRACK process is all about recognising this thinking as being the cause of your angry reaction, rather than the event.

We can't change what we don't acknowledge, so this is the first step to changing your anger. What you will find once you recognise this thinking is that straight away you've noticed that you are in conflict with reality and, already, that will lessen the intensity of your emotions.

There is absolutely no point in allowing that should've/could've conversation to keep rolling around in your head. This will only cause further stress. The only way to change how you feel is to accept the reality of life's events, which brings us to our next step on the TRACK process – REALITY.

HOW TO PUT TODAY'S LESSON INTO PRACTICE

What is it that you are thinking that has got you all riled up?

First, practice staying aware of how you feel – the emotions that you are experiencing (i.e. anger).

Try to catch the thoughts that were going through your mind to create that feeling and recognise how they are in conflict with reality.

(PLEASE NOTE: you won't be able to catch all of your thoughts. We think about 70,000 thoughts a day, so let your feelings be your indicators that there are conflicting thoughts going on causing these emotions.)

Read more at ParentalStress.com.au

Follow us on Facebook:
facebook.com/parentalstresscentre

DAY 24
COME BACK TO REALITY.
STEP 2 OF THE MIND TRACK TO
HAPPINESS PROCESS

Having recognised your thinking that is in resistance to your new unwanted reality, you now need to bring yourself into alignment with accepting the present situation, just as it is.

In week two, I gave you several ways to do this. I will summarise them here to help you to implement this step:

Find the hidden good in the bad –
How does this event hold value? Even though we didn't get what we want, we still received an experience of value.

- They either teach us something directly – how to 'do' life differently (event learning: how do we know what to do until we experience what NOT to do).

- They teach us about ourselves and how we want life to be.

- They can give us information that we didn't know before that helps us experience other events.

- The unwanted event leads to another event that we found beneficial (for example, my struggles led me to my mother's group which I adore).

Look at the bigger picture –

Widen back from directly focussing on the present moment, and look for what this present moment means from a larger perspective.

- The reality is we all experience ups and downs, wanted and unwanted events.

- This too shall pass – Everything rises and passes away. Nothing lasts forever.

- We all learn, grow and develop at different ages and stages (where is your child developmentally? Do they physically have the capabilities that you are expecting of them? Will this stage eventually pass on due to learning, growth and maturity?)

- Things come and go, only to come back again – a house gets clean and then gets dirty; washing gets done and put away, only to come back again; children are happy, then have cranky days – just like me.

Experience the anger –

Everything is energy. So are our thoughts and our emotions. When you are feeling angry, it is because the energy of your thoughts is creating the energy of your emotions. The more your thinking is resisting whatever is happening, the more you increase the energy of your anger.

Energy always has to go somewhere. It needs to be expressed. Rather than it leading to an outburst, allow yourself to experience the emotion of anger, just as it is – without judgement and without resistance.

Feel what it feels like to have this emotion we label as anger. Where does it start in the body? Where does it stop? Where are its edges? How deep does it go? What is this feeling actually like? What you'll be doing when you are focussing on this feeling is allowing it to be acknowledged and expressed, without any actions or words needed.

PLEASE NOTE: don't do this with the desire for your anger to hurry up and go, as this is still you being in resistance. You MUST experience it just as it is, without judgement, and allow it to rise and pass away.

My self-worth cannot be compromised –

If self-worth was defined only by achievement, success, well-behaved children, how good we are at things or someone else's opinion of us, NONE OF US would be worthy.

Your true worth comes from your existence. You are here as a human being doing the best that you know how to do with the information you have and making the best decisions you know how to make in each moment. By doing this, you are contributing to everyone who comes in contact with you and are providing an arena for them to experience, learn and grow in their lives too.

We all play a valuable part in the unfolding of life and there is NOTHING you need to do, be or have to make you more or less worthy than you already are. You are ALREADY 100% WORTHY!!

The above four categories are the fundamentals for you being able to bring your attention back into alignment with reality.

Of course, they are just the fundamentals. The application of these points may need to be taken through a more intense dissection in regards to your specific circumstances and the events occurring in your life.

Please know that I am here to support you through change and that I have multiple products that can directly help further your learning of this information in the context of your unique circumstances. Come and visit my website, www.ParentalStress.com.au, to find out more.

For now, however, let's look at how to put this lesson into practice...

HOW TO PUT TODAY'S LESSON INTO PRACTICE

Bring your thinking back into alignment with reality:

FIRST, the reality of what is ACTUALLY happening; and SECOND, the reality of the bigger picture of life and your intrinsic self-worth.

- *Find the hidden good in the bad where possible.*

- *Look at life's highs and lows, unwanted and wanted events, as a normal part of life.*

- *Look for how your child is learning, growing and developing.*

- *Leave your self-worth out of the events in your life –*
  your worth is irrelevant to any life event.

- *Experience your anger just as it is, without judgement.*

Finally, this step is all about ACCEPTING THE CURRENT MOMENT. You don't have to like your reality, but you do need to accept it.

In Step 3, we will shift your focus towards changing your reality for the future through AIM.

Read more at ParentalStress.com.au

Follow us on Facebook:
facebook.com/parentalstresscentre

DAY 25
AIM FOR WHAT YOU DO WANT. STEP 3 OF THE MIND TRACK TO HAPPINESS PROCESS

Just because you accept your reality, doesn't mean you won't want to change your reality. Step Three of the Mind TRACK to Happiness Process gets you solution-focussed!

Rather than focussing on what you aren't getting or what is going 'wrong', we are now shifting your focus to what you want. What is the ideal of this situation?

Before you begin to do this, however, you first need to understand what exactly a goal is and what the true purpose of a goal is.

What is a Goal?

A goal is anything that you set out to do. They don't have to be big goals or long-term goals. Goals can be as simple as getting out of bed in a morning, or brushing your teeth.

That would mean, from this perspective, we are ALWAYS setting goals.

What is the True Purpose of Goals?

A common misconception of goals is that we need to achieve them in order to be valuable as a person, or to get my life to go 'right' (i.e. have a successful or valuable life).

However, although we will always set goals in order to achieve them, the reality is that we don't always achieve them because life doesn't always go to plan.

Incidentally, achieving goals is not even their true PURPOSE.

The true purpose of setting goals is to SET LIFE IN MOTION.

When we set a goal, we participate in life. We have experiences. We learn and grow and we then contribute that knowledge and those experiences to other people around us, thus contributing to their journeys through life.

Hence, it's not actually about getting to the goal at all (even though we'd like to achieve all our goals). We learn through the experiences we have on our way towards the goal, when we get to the goal and also when we don't get to our goals.

All of it is valuable, not just the part where we get what we want. And because we are always learning and contributing a part of ourselves to other people, and contributing to their lives, we are always 100% worthy and valuable.

Goals do not define your self-worth. The reality is that sometimes I get what I want and sometimes I don't. Refer to the REALITY step for how to align with the reality of unwanted events (e.g. finding the hidden good in the bad).

How to Set My AIM

Now we have that out of the way and there's nothing you need to achieve in order to be a more valuable parent or person (because you are always doing your best and contributing the best way you know how, right now), let's focus on what it is you actually want.

When setting your AIM, you need to consider the following questions:

- What do I want? What is the ideal of this situation?

- Is it specific? (Can I measure my progress? Will I know once I have achieved it?)

- Is what I want in conflict with reality? (Is it realistic? Is it possible given the current circumstances?)

- Will I actually achieve my goal or is it a constant work in progress? (e.g. my child's behaviour or my ability to remain calm throughout chaos)

- Why do I want this AIM? (Have I incorrectly attached my self-worth to the achievement of this goal?)

Once you have established what your specific goal is - and are confident that you are not setting yourself up to be in conflict with reality or that you have attached your self-worth to the achievement of your goal - then you are ready to move onto the fourth step of the Mind TRACK to Happiness Process – CHOICES.

HOW TO PUT TODAY'S LESSON INTO PRACTICE

Remember these important points about goals before you actually set your AIM:

- *A goal is anything you set out to achieve.*

- *Sometimes we don't achieve the goals that we set, but we ALWAYS receive an experience that holds value (find the hidden good in the bad).*

- *Goals simply set life in motion and allow you to experience, learn, grow and contribute to yours and others' journeys through life.*

- *Goals do NOT define self-worth.*

- *The value comes from the experiences and learning you get on the way to your goal, when you get your goal and when you don't get your goal.*

How to set your AIM checklist – Is my AIM......

- *Specific?*

- *Realistic?*

- *Measurable?*

- *Aligned with reality?*

- *Not attached to my self-worth?*

Read more at ParentalStress.com.au

Follow us on Facebook: facebook.com/parentalstresscentre

DAY 26

CHOICES: HOW DO I GET WHAT I WANT? STEP 4 OF THE MIND TRACK TO HAPPINESS PROCESS

It's often too easy to get sucked into denial or resistance over what is going on in your life. I mean, it's one thing to set your AIM, but sometimes we have absolutely no clue how to get to that goal. If you did, then you would be doing it and moving towards your goal.

But therein lies the whole point of life. We don't know everything and life sends us in directions where we don't know what to do. But what happens when we're challenged? We are forced to learn!!

This step teaches you to grab the reins of your life and learn your way through your problems by deliberately seeking out the information you need to make the necessary changes - changes that will not only move you past your problems, but move you closer to your AIM.

If you are experiencing a challenging stage with your child, rather than complain and get angry over it occurring, accept the reality that this is just another part of your parenting experience (and another part of your child's development). Start looking for how you and your child can move through this stage quicker.

It may mean looking up parenting resources, seeking out experts in that particular area of the challenge, asking other parents, sitting down and hearing what's happening for your child and brainstorming solutions with them or simply being aware that you have to just ride the storm (remember everything rises and passes away).

If you are experiencing relationship problems, seek out information that will teach you communication skills, how to negotiate, how to put the fire back in the relationship, etc.

If you are experiencing financial difficulties, seek out professionals who have a wealth of knowledge in the area of accumulating money, people who have been in your shoes, or parents who have been able to make money or save money on just one income. You could also read books on how to earn money or become part of forums connecting with people who have the same goals.

Deliberately seek out people who can educate you on how to move towards your financial goals. If you knew how to do it, you'd already be doing it, so why not deliberately seek out the information that will teach you how?

We only know what we know at any given moment, and sometimes what we know is not enough to help us through our challenges. We must learn.

This is not you failing. This is you living! This is you being a learning, growing, developing human being who doesn't know everything there is to know about life. This is you being just like everyone else. We all get challenged and we all have to learn and grow from these challenges.

Being a parent, we are often indoctrinated to believe that we should know all there is to know about raising children, however, we have not raised our children before. Even if you have gone through the same stage with your older children, each child is unique and may need a different approach.

Treat each challenge with your kids, or in any other area, as an opportunity to learn more about how to handle life. You may not enjoy the challenge and what's happening, but you need to accept it. If you set an AIM for where you would like to head now that you are experiencing your current unwanted reality, and start deliberately seeking out answers, then you will learn how to move past your challenges a lot quicker.

HOW TO PUT TODAY'S
LESSON INTO PRACTICE

It's time to get solution-focussed about how to get what you want!!

Who can educate you on how to deal with your present challenges and move you towards your AIM?

Seek out information from the internet, experts in that topic, friends, family, forums, books, magazines, videos, workshops or any other resource that offers knowledge about what you are challenged by.

Look for people who have walked in your shoes and use them for support. Learn from them with the understanding that you have not failed for not already knowing this information. You are simply experiencing an event and you require more information.

So get out there and find the information you need without feeling like a failure.

Read more at ParentalStress.com.au

Follow us on Facebook:
facebook.com/parentalstresscentre

DAY 27

KNOW YOUR PLAN & ACTION IT. THE FINAL STEP OF <u>THE MIND TRACK TO HAPPINESS PROCESS</u>

I remember when I first came across the power of accepting your reality then turning your attention towards becoming solution-focussed.

My youngest son Ryan was just two and a half years old when he began his tantrums. At first I was okay with them because I was aligned with the reality of them just being 'a phase'.

But when that 'phase' began to last over a year in length, well, let's just say that became quite taxing on my ability to keep my cool.

I knew I had to do something about it.

So, as per each step of the Mind TRACK to Happiness Process, I accepted the REALITY of where Ryan was in his development, set my AIM to teach him how to learn a different approach to not getting what he wants and made the CHOICE to seek out information on how I could handle his tantrums differently.

I struggle to remember now what the actual technique was that I decided to use, but I do remember how I felt when I had decided to use this new technique.

I HAD A PLAN.

And because I had a plan, I was ready for his tantrums. So ready, in fact, it was almost as if I became impatient as I waited for his next tantrum to occur. I wanted to use my new technique. So when he threw his next tantrum, I was far from angry over it. I was almost (but not quite) excited about my new plan and the potential solution it could bring.

This is the power of having a plan. You know what it is that you are going to do to tackle your problems and you begin moving towards your AIM.

In the fourth step of the TRACK process, CHOICES, you armed yourself with information on how to get what you want. In this final step, KNOW YOUR PLAN & ACTION IT, you now want to formulate your information into an action plan that you can follow and use to measure your progress.

When dealing with a behavioural technique, write down each step of that technique so you remember what to do.

If you are dealing with a financial goal, write down which steps you are going to implement in which order to start moving forward.

If you are dealing with an AIM to change certain aspects of your behaviour (like becoming a calm mother or father), create some affirmations, use the resources that have been teaching you what to do – like *The Happy Mum Handbook* – and create an ACTION plan to keep you moving in that direction.

It's important to understand that getting to this point in the TRACK process does not mean your life is fixed. This is because your life is not broken. Problems are only indicators that something needs to be learnt. If you treat them that way, problems do not become problems, just opportunities to get more information on how to 'do' life better.

You will be at various stages of this Mind TRACK to Happiness Process in different areas of your life at different times. Often, you may get a little stuck in the THOUGHTS part before you are ready to accept REALITY and continue with the last three solution-focussed steps – AIM, CHOICES and KNOW YOUR PLAN & ACTION IT.

There is no right or wrong way for your life to unfold. There are just experiences. Some of them you will like, and some of them you will not.

The ones you don't like are necessary for providing you with an arena for learning. The quicker you are able to treat your problems in that way and deliberately seek out the lessons you need to move past them, the quicker you will get back onto that TRACK to Happiness and feel a lot more peace in your life.

HOW TO PUT TODAY'S
LESSON INTO PRACTICE

Gather the information that you found in step four – CHOICES - and begin putting together an ACTION plan for moving towards your goals.

Know that each challenge that occurs in your life is just a new phase of learning and that challenges occur to force you into learning about life and about yourself.

Read more at ParentalStress.com.au

Follow us on Facebook:
facebook.com/parentalstresscentre

DAY 28
CONGRATULATIONS! YOU MADE IT! HERE'S WHAT TO DO NEXT....

Congratulations!

You have made it to the 28th day of our Tame Your Temper Parenting Challenge.

I'm sure you've had your highs and lows throughout this challenge. I know that I have!!

But as you've also learnt – that is life.

This is how we learn, by experiencing something challenging and dropping the ball every once and a while (or a lot).

If you've gotten to this part of the challenge, then I want you to congratulate yourself for a job well done. It doesn't matter if you still yelled here or there. It doesn't matter if you still wouldn't consider yourself to be a parent with a tamed temper.

The important part is that you tried and you learnt some more information about how to think differently and avoid getting angry in the future.

Stopping your anger is not about stopping the event. It's about recognising the thoughts that have created that sensation in the body that we label as anger. It's about experiencing and releasing that energy, then changing your thoughts to be in alignment with reality.

The 28 Day **TAME YOUR TEMPER** CHALLENGE

The beauty of having participated in this challenge is that you can now repeat the challenge over and over again, as needed, because you now have the information on how to change.

And just like when you learnt to walk, talk and use a spoon, repetition of this information will continue to teach you how to habitually think and respond to the ups and downs of all aspects of your life.

Please take some time to recognise the wins that you have had on this challenge and the obvious effects that you have found it has had on your family, too.

This challenge has given you a taste of what *The Parental Stress Centre of Australia* teaches and I hope that you have been able to take away something that has changed you forever.

Changing a habit can be difficult, and if anger is something that seems to come easy to you (as it used to with me as well), you may find it beneficial to know that you can learn more information on how to change through other products I have written.

Perhaps your tendency to yell comes from a much deeper sadness about yourself and your life or is a result of depression or anxiety that may be lurking.

The Parental Stress Centre of Australia specialises in resources that will help you deal with these personal issues in the context of being a mother and learn more about how to change your mindset and turn your life around.

At a basic level, *The Happy Mum Handbook*, will teach you how to stop and prevent motherhood stress, depression and anxiety.

However, on a deeper level, products such as the 4-part webinar series: *How to End Motherhood Stress and Depression*' and *The Postpartum Depression Recovery Program* both offer a more personalised analysis and SUPPORT from me on how to understand your unique stress, depression and/or anxiety and how to change. With both of these products, I personally help you to apply this information to your specific circumstances while you learn the information.

And dads, don't worry. This information, although directed at mums, provides information that can help and support you to change too, just like this challenge has done.

All of my products come with a money-back guarantee, because I firmly believe that if I can't help you, then I don't want your money. So there is never anything to lose and everything to gain.

But for now, however, it is time to let you loose from your daily lessons and leave you to continue enjoying the benefits of applying the information you've already learnt.

Please continue to be kind to yourself and remember that you are always 100% worthy. I believe that today's parents – mothers, specifically – are stuck in between a generation of old school: 'stay at home and do everything for your kids' and new school: 'you can have the world and be everything to your kids too'.

This can be confusing, so stay true to yourself, enjoy the good times, knowing that they will also rise and pass away, and approach the hard times with the knowledge that this is just an experience for you to learn and grow from. No event can define your self-worth.

Just take each event as it comes and remember to use the five steps of the Mind TRACK to Happiness Process to allow the reality of life's ups and downs to flow – events coming in and events going out (just like the air going in and the air going out).

Nothing is permanent, and neither will your anger be permanent. With repetition and consistency, you WILL change to be the happy, calm mum or dad you have set out to be.

I wish you the very best in your future.

Lots of love and happiness,

Jackie Hall
www.ParentalStress.com.au

Lightning Source UK Ltd.
Milton Keynes UK
UKOW01f0808011117
311997UK00010B/413/P